# THE ENORMOUS CHORUS

FRANK KUENSTLER

# The Enormous Chorus

INTRODUCTION BY MICHAEL O'BRIEN

PRESSED WAFER | BOSTON | 2011

This selection was made from the following books:

*Selected Poems* (New York: Eventorium Press, 1964)
*Paradise News* (New York: Eventorium Press, 1966)
*Fugitives. Rounds* (New York: Eventorium Press, 1966)
*13½ Poems* (New York: SZ/Press, 1984)
*Continued* (New York: Nine Three Press, 1987)
*The Seafarer, B.Q.E., and Other Poems*
     (New York: Cairn Editions, 1996)

PRESSED WAFER
9 Columbus Square, Boston, Massachusetts 02116

Printed in the United States

# CONTENTS

# INTRODUCTION

Frank Kuenstler's "Canto 33" opens

*In medias res, the human voice, crystal,*

making a kind of rubric: three propositions at the outset of something said, or, better, Duke Ellington laying out the terms of a song. *In medias res* comes from Horace: "in the midst of the thing," the place where we begin a story, a day, between a beginning we can't remember and the end which is an end to all remembering. Here. Now. In what Wallace Stevens calls "The the." And what we find, in all this immediacy, this perpetual ongoing middle, is *the human voice*. The poems show a constant appetite for it, for engaging with its unbroken rivers of talk. And that voice is *crystal*: "clear as crystal," as we say, but also "a structure consisting of periodically repeated, identically constructed congruent unit cells." (This sounds like a description of *Lens*, his first, most radical book.) To crystallize is "to take on definite and permanent form." Granted the way his mind worked, crystal is also probably not far from a crystal set, a radio housing voices, nor from Stendhal's *On Love*, in which crystallization is the process of an emotion finding its form.

A lot of work for seven words, and with a rhyme as well. But consider the associative processes that run these poems, their density of reference, the swiftness of their transitions. The internet works like this, all interacting simultaneities. And the glue that holds it all together is human speech:

*The world hangs by a thread of verbs & nouns.*

The poems' openness to the overtones of words is unfailing, sometimes to the exclusion of their everyday workhorse lives. The point was to find a way to bring that abundance to bear in the moment of the poem. Many poets proceed by cutting out the overload; he tried to make room for it. He didn't write as if English were in a museum, and he didn't write to put it there. Poetry was, by its nature, provisional; that's why he wrote so much of it. He was steadily intelligent but not at all high-minded; if puns were good enough for Joyce, they were good enough for him. Likewise gobbledygook—"trying to talk to Mama," as he once described it. He was discerning without prejudice: junk had its uses—cartoons, cheesy movies, newspaper headlines. To move between the sublime and the ridiculous, as he did, programmatically, all the time, and with great rapidity, wasn't a blunder—they were parts of the same terrain. He never treated his materials with superiority, though often with compounded ironies. There is great sadness and anger in some of the poems, and sometimes a blank opacity more troubling than either. But, inexhaustibly, there is something like joy at the level of language.

Sometimes he says it into being:

> *If summer is the image of a string of pearls*
> *There is music everywhere.*

where assertion does the work of discovery. Other times the world is not posited but simply, or not so simply, given as found. For his findings were seldom simple. Simplicity surprised him, as it surprises us when it turns up in the poems.

One mustn't leave out how funny they are, how much pleasure they give, how responsive their quickness—"Who runs may read." At their best, as, say, in "Blind Ossian Addresses the Sun Again," their reach is immense. Over and over inchoate feelings take shape, change, move on. Fixity is rare in them, something stale and lifeless. It often seems as if he were doing six things at once, changing trains and levels of thought as he speaks: more than one person is talking, and all at once. Precarious to negotiate such a Babel. The stakes of the poems were very high: to come to some kind of terms with the rich, rolling chaos of the world, make something commensurate with it. What they do is this:

> *Praise what was ordered a second in the mind*

\*

Hard to make a selection of the poems of someone whose every impulse was for inclusion. Much remains to be done. A reprint of *Lens*—for the book defies editing—is the next thing needed. Then manuscripts need to be looked at—this selection draws only on the books that he published. *The Rabbi Kyoto Poems* should be gathered and published, and *The Baseball Book*, meant to secure his old age. Friends should be consulted: sometimes the post office was his publisher. He was abundant.

There is good news: tapes of two of his readings can be found at PennSound (http://writing.upenn.edu/pennsound/x/Kuenstler.html), likewise five of the films, restored by Anthology Film Archives; his last two books, *In Which* and *The Seafarer, B.Q.E., and Other Poems*, are available from Cairn Editions (jcfmob@verizon .net). But time passes. When Lady Murasaki is asked by the Prince why she writes she says *So there will never be a time when people don't know these things happened.* His work should not be lost.

MICHAEL O'BRIEN

## A NOTE ON THE TEXT

Oddities of spelling, capitalization, and punctuation herein are present in the sources as well. The poet was aware of what he called "the tragicomedy of punctuation", but considered some mistakes worth making and was at least tolerant of others. He was not in the business of providing models of orthography or other versions of good housekeeping. Sometimes he deliberately roughens up the surface of a poem. He believed in keeping faith with the world's disorder. There are problems, but

> *the book*
> *like the body, is no problem.*

# THE ENORMOUS CHORUS

## PROMETHEUS

Flesh, too, those birds that peck at him
& bite. They're black as night. The sky
is blue, unscarred & South Caucasian.
He lives & dies upon a bed of rock,
hears his cry, "The revolution is dead!
Long live it!" echo like the lament
of a now near-mad aristocrat whose
slaves have been freed by an imperial
edict. Chains invisible as nails on a
well-made coffin are wrought by his spirit,
a spirit perverse, I say, mouthing freedoms
which later on may prove unreal. But,
like a fool, this I must think about
some more, at leisure. Meanwhile, his
entrails burn. Their flames attract
the magpies, vultures, sparrows, all the
birds, as if he were a renegade, or an
ineffectual scarecrow. His eyes filmed
over, through them the rocks appear wrapped
in cellophane. Unreal images, monuments
of their kind, they, like the birds, speak
no evil. Nor do I. I have seen & read
the signs. My trademark's fire.
"Dark it grows & dark," Prometheus says.
The air begins to clear. He has prayed
this day for darkness. We inherit
the epicycle, nuance, dance & drama of his year.

POEM

Neoclassicism is pornographic. The two
guns are impotent. Both.
A magazine is half the globe.
Man is not a cipher. He travels by signs.
Sale is the practice of alienation.
A poem is something that happens twice.
Love is the repetition of love.
Trotsky harangues the Peace Conference
in Paradise.
*Je vous en pris.* Massacred
into another pair of trousers
the blue chip number, Poetry
revolves about its axis the guise
of hypnosis, the Cosmological Casino,
the causal canal connecting
heredity & the Mediterranean.
The Dancer discurses the Swan, the Train
the Bard-on-the-Boards
a theatre of vaudeville between her armpits,
her "grandes chats" pirouettes
a monocle of spirit, a silver silhouette.
At the trough of numbers, members feed
the Moon's flight, & Sun's inconstant need.

## PROSERPINE'S GARDEN

In the print upon my wall
A girl has flowers in her hair.
She holds a flowered hat
As if she had a reason.
A vase of flowers is beside her, too.

A vase of flowers is beside me, too.
Unpictured & unframed,
As befits my passion.
Hell is every season.
Spring is in the air.

In Proserpine's garden many choruses
Are bunched to sing Spring's cost of rape
& many marriages. The price of promises
They cry, by footfall to florist,
A cut flower at a time. Over & over, but
Never well.

The bowl can't hold their withering.
They can't keep up their heads. "Overripe!"
They cry, descending, mouth to mouth pay,
Stem to stem, in Hades' arms
Of musclebound harness,
In the arms of his musclebound cell.

2.

In the winter garden there's the racket
Of anguish on each statue's face,
Snow everywhere, a thin, comfortless

Blanket of it, & a pool
Of studied clay. The paradise sky
Divines its two roles, plays halo

& mistletoe both, alternately both.

## MOON POISED

The way to justify a paged sigh is to reincarnate the man in the moon. O Solomon, wert thou were alive in this hour, master of Sheba! The snows cascaded down the footnote. The wind blew, "Four o'clock." Everything was still, the same as you remember, only different. And the difference was this, that whereas before we could only type two words to a page, now— ever since July 4th—we can manage six or seven. And that's good news. Because with the additional words on the line, more words affix to the page.

To continue: the footnote at the bottom of the page is a smile. Red or black as the case may be. Depends on the color of snow at that time of the year. And the shape of the book, of course. Now you know. And when the moon shifts a degree off its axis, all is lost.

spelled cantos. "All is lost."

*Asterisks are footnotes at the bottom of the page.* This way or that. The footnote, in any case, spells the difference. Now you know. And that's good news. Precisely the news we were awaiting, when Solomon's chariot, bearing Sheba, came advancing upon the scene. And stopped the clocks. And stopped the snow. And made our moustache disappear.

moon poised

Like a blue & white black icicle.

And the heart of the matter is this: if the clocks didn't stop forever, our moustache'd never disappear.

## 1927

sunrise. Surprise. In medias res
the dance of life begins. The Golden Harp
sings in the Happy Valley. A picture
of a flower just flashed upon
the screen. My son, beware.
The Jazz Age began in 1919
with the May Day riots of that year.
There's a mambo step called 1987.
Some crabgrass mugged a cartoon
crocus in the park. It must be Spring.
It might as well. The king's gone hunting
for the thous & rooks in the queen's diadem.
When he was 61, on his birthday,
Bojangles Robinson danced up Broadway
from 42nd to 125th Streets. In the movie
*Broadway*, Hollywood created its own B'way.
jiggernaut! chardas! songspiel! The
Warsaw Uprising coincided with the
historical Passover. The mambo & the horse's
step are one. The bomb over Hiroshima
was nicknamed Gilda. The rhumba
is a development of the waltz.
In Cuba-Oriente Xmas-trees are turned to waltzes.
& built the pyramids. & launched a thousand rockettes.
Might as well. 33 hours in the air. "*Oui.*"
joy. Illusion. 1933. Lindy-Hope. Blues.
Six million unemployed. Beware, my
son. Despair the twin & virgin,
the plebian hero & rich man's son. Johnny Reb
asleep at the side of Lenin. Wrong-way Coughlin.
scarface. *Mickey*. Cohen. There *is* no Northwest
Passage! When the Nazi gunmen
were cast out of the city of Vienna,
mad glad Nijinsky danced in its downtown streets.
Leopold served 33 years, went South to flourish.
Wean! cry uncool! Beware, my son, beware,
the grapes of the fruit of jazz, secret
film, silent film, *sich* idiom,
& especially, the fiction of the 'forties.

## CANTO 33

In medias res, the human voice, crystal,
the voice of imitation begins. And Paris
& Rome are twin cities, as if, firfin & polis,
Sagittarius were winged & wrought, a dragon,
a democratic centaur cartoon. I live
in twin cities, & remember Alcibiades. At noon
the city & the sirens sing. And who lives
in twin cities, "the best frigate in the world
is a good book," I read. "A child has never
wept nor slain a thousand kin," Dutch Schultz,
dying, said. God invented chronology, but
"the Revolution cut Time in half," according
to Trotsky. Twin Gemini houses the seasons
& hours, an insupportable crown to an
insupportable universe. & Late & soon I will
lay me down, & ear to the ground hear news
of our era, tales of the St. Valentine's Day-
St. Bartholemew's Eve murder. Like Jesuit
saints, they fled. Murdered & free, they marched.
A storm-lot & terrible, they cursed. And
forty dancing angels fled like thieves.
I live in twin cities, Gnome & Moscow, with
a bust of Shakespeare & Cervantes, midst
degrees of difference, right & wrong (in Ardennes
& Eden: andantes), amazing double-breasted
images. "I saw her walking toward me. In her hand
she carried a flower. She was a dancer.
O how I loved her!" Adam in Athens photographed
her hard by the Argive Sea, against the skies' ruins.
They echoed, "Remember me!" The whole world must
remember. Molière was an actor. Crime is natural. The
gods are vengeful. Did we fall! . . . I take the workshop
cure. If Marx were alive today! . . . Jesus! Gautier!
There are apple blossoms falling, printing presses
rolling. I can swing my head like a lantern,
ice-skate in Italy italically; free, as Everyman
once caught hanging like a dagger from a tree.

SNOW

Myrna Loy, the good Bette Davis, the dream's anthology
a thousand & a million schoolgirls sigh
& so do I, as if
Fred Astaire were the only white man in the universe
Gable's ears, Sammy Davis' ghost, Sinatra's spats
the man not quite lost in the Automat washroom
after his splendid Longchamps repast
rinsing his skeleton choppers (teeth, between you & me)
removed, in place again, as a urinal flushed
like a bad joke's echo that'll haunt every pastoral
& reverie. Movies, they say, are like roses, dreams,
fictions, artifacts, food, & I agree. I have, it seems
been chewing the placenta eons & centuries nigh
years without number divided by two into programs
as if each were a vivid prosepoem or a true translation
& strung I've been, as once induced & stung, & stay
still a dragon, not strong but determined
from the past sky to the momentary, monumental
televised, walking washing machine. Just once!
a chisel! an axe! to be armed again, figleaf
intact! The Southwest desert, alias Achilles' shield
would roll in my palm like the Green Giant
Gawain's friend. Two poems I'd guess
infinite & perfect, gem-like G-Man's balls
despite the dust of the empyrean! Alas
I swoon. From dawn's authority, the studio, sans trappings
I was always out on loan. And every mistake's called
human, like months of the year named after women
& the eight-minute dance, umbilical, & proverbial
On the floor of the cutting room
Hollywood! Babylon! England! Laocoon! cry of joy & paean!

# VALENTINE

(Homage to Lou by G.A., Respectfully Passionate)

Leaning out to the wide seaside garden lifted like a breast
Perched over the abyss I dominate the ocean like a master

I salute you Lou like your favorite tree the palm
Your hair like spilled blood
To die at last and know the luring of Eternity
Olive trees waved at times just as her lashes do

Through this book which is firm & precise in its joy
Learn O Lou to know me so as never to forget me
As even in spite of you I am putting down here
Your most secret thoughts, God's assigned regards.

# APPLEBAUM'S SONG TO LOLA MONTEZ

My name is Applebaum. Call me my Lincoln.
I'll write you a neo-play. "And how
did you enjoy the conditions of tragedy, Mrs. M?"
It's Dali's theory
that our Lady Mona Leica beguiled the camerilla,
& *after the painting by de Kostrowitz*
it's the paper that counts.
"Balls!" said the Queen. the King, angel of Dee,
smiled. He had to
& ms/LST, before Lucky Strike green
went to war,
the moral equivalent of A-trees, I guess,
where, before, Adam & Eve were wont to wander,
gather for food hand in hand in Eden together,
"the land is sterile & bare,
as if passed over by a razor."
The Red Sea's curtains like a theatre parted.
A press agent farted & saved the day,
an actress, where the blue & green beguine.
Not in between. My name is legion.
My name is Applebaum. My name is nemesis.
My name is Weiss. Red flags photograph black.
"The drama is a mystery, not a form."
I froze, therefore, I am.

According to HG, who knows, pieta
the lord is an engine of war. Who travels
lonely as a crowd: "a rogues' gallery of vice-presidents,"
& the first screening of *Potemkin* in the US
was on Gloria Swanson's bedsheet.
Who also ran, moniker, but not for me,
a lark is not a lark, a tree is not a tree,
a house is not a house, "Shoot it in Griffith Park!"
More wars waltz whores, not parks,
to the tune of '33. & a third.
It only laughs when I hurt. I stink,
therefore I am. It's good to be alive.
I'm sorry I wrote this poem. My best to Uncle Sam.
My regards to Uncle Tom.

My name is Applebaum. My name is lesion.
My name is nem. Isis. My name is Christ.
The nearest exist: Dance of Life.
shivas. Riga. pumpkins. slippers. Snakeyes. Dice.
iamb. IX. My name is *Sunset*. stern. ML&M. Lincoln.
Tricolor. Tobacco. Tattoo. Hindustan.
Cannes-Cannes. cuba-Klan. cut. Rain. vibes.
cuneiform. Tijeans. aplomb. Khan-Khan.
wives. legs. diamonds. Biely. Lives.
Yes, dear friends, Biely lives
day/Lay. Pleasurism & pornography are twins,
& kinKatz sings
Applebaum's Song to Lola Montez.

# BLIND OSSIAN ADDRESSES THE SUN AGAIN

A day of snow on the Riviera, the burlesque queens
are mermaids, simple as the moon. Another New Year's
Day in Havana, without discourse, they who cul-
tivated the dimensions of their bodies, like lizards
are regimented as our shadows. That's bad news,
The natural gambler opined. A traveller on the steps of Odessa
  in distress & the going is hard & slow,
   Enormous snowflakes stripped as the voice you know.

  I should really be writing a letter to everybody
saying what I mean. I mean the bodies are blonde, brown
as sunshine, while my feet are cold. There is no news
  in the world for us, only images grasped at, or fed us
  like straws. The possible dimensions are what remind
Us that we were born once upon a time, & yelled like dawn.
   The gamblers have moved south to oil & coffee country.
  The television sets up north transmit pictures.
  Snow is socialized. A rumor persists
  that estimates of the life of the sun have been wildly exaggerated.
  In the thirties it was Egypt & the other Alexandria
You cannot know.

   I will walk in the snow & get my feet wet. I will go
to the movies. I will hope. The bloody braille of the sun
is my tongue. The king was executed just because he thought
  he could be happy. He enjoyed his job. He enjoyed
  having his friends around. He enjoyed having money.
He enjoyed Marilyn Monroe, if such a thing was possible.
  Degree by degree I went blind, thinking of the sun in Havana,
  thinking its eye was as narrow & wide as a pair of hips.

I will walk in Autumn. The Eiffel Tower will greet me, tell
  me in Turkish the way to Afghanistan. Apollinaire & Vergil
  will guide me, because I am blind, the way to the Far East
  dimension of the world's highway, O South
  The way musicians named Ossian have always been led by clarinets
& apprentice butchers since the world was young.

# ORPHEUS & ANARCHY

### 1. TWENTY EDITORIALS

The next necessary thing is television. "What cannot be bought is the character of the species." Some days the NY Times reads like a comic strip. What cannot be bought is the character of the specious. The Eichmann Trial was a comedy. Maybe the Negroes will solve the Negro Question. They will not, however, save us all. The most effective myth, power, is not necessarily Christian. Maybe the Negroes will solve the Negro Question. Manner, grotesquerie, tic, style, understood: dialect.Tits, the Jewish Question is a woman.

All the analysts are wrong. Drunks asleep on the sidewalk pavement—effective pastoral—are talking about the totality of existence. "Resume domestic relations with Cuba," they say. "Better read than dead." "Resurrection!" In any case, the war situation should permit us to ask ourselves what do we want to live for, and the vista (horizon) of power without guilt, that possibility perverted by it would seem only carriers, the Cold Warriors, is, as it's been for a century, still indicated, tho hardly ever mentioned, and would seem at least the only possibly serious entertainment.

Figleaves: those halos, laurels.

The esthetic of the first dimension, read anyway.

A revolutionary journalism of forms.

kharma.Dei.

I would like to take this opportunity to say:

The Chronicles of Kennedy was written by Stendhal. Yet we continue to ejaculate in the direction of some kind of salvation.

## 2. PROMETHEUS ELECT

Chained as I am to the typewriter, I might
as well be chained to hope. I'm not Snow White.
I'm the radical dope. Poor Marilyn!
She took so seriously the culture that now
rolls like Easter eggs on the White House lawn.
That's all right. We took seriously a doctrine.
Once, tempted & mistaken, she thought
she was married to Lincoln. A brief, historic
monument, biped, it was only Henry Fonda
married to a Chrysler, for a song. *Foolish
as a bluebird.* It was the dawn. I'll build a fire
to keep us warm. *She was a daughter of the
working-class, not of our Empire. We ought
to have loved her more.* I am a Marxist. I am
a democrat. I am a socialist. I am a whore.
& every fucking movie-star, producer, director, editor,
psychoanalyst, journalist, president, pressagent & entrepreneur.

### 3. The Pagan God

(Eye & Voice)

Having witnessed the latest type performed,
a committee operation, in this amphitheatre,
I awoke drunk, on a shelf, in a cave. For-
maldehyde categories, pertinent & correct,
escape my cross-eyed gaze. (It is, in paren-
thesis, all too simple, sober & circumspect.)
Here, the maze once seen, is roundly locked,
a crystal instrument. Or flesh. Nose-
like, it's rubbed, then rolls in dirt. Unable
to move, I at least perceive the order of A-
jax's wheel that was my dying command. My
x-ray eyes, my singed hair, my mantle of air
crowds me, punishing once mighty joints
& limbs. And I see you, within, cave
within cave, my daughter, working like hell,
getting the musical comedy ready for Spring.

4.

kingsaw. As bad as his word.
To resist is to feed.
Evil is the principle of negation.
The cracked mirror echoes constructs.
The mirror echoes shadows
& voices. Man strives
for the invisible, inevitable & unreal.
Up the intellectual, Apollonian-Faustian man!
More fiction, naturalism: Oliver Twist's song!

### 5. Poem for the Memory of Myself

        saga. Nevermore.
        the bust of Shakespeare.
        blake. Bird.

I wandered lonely on Crusades
tracking down a Vth
for Ulysses S. Grant

my Civil War
a call for sponsors.
This age, my friends, is one of fish

& myth
"Join or die!" they said. I died, belabored.

6. Labyrinth

That perfect olive being has drowned.
The map of the world is round
each stitch embroidered on a handkerchief,
a sigh, a star & scarf.

Heroes are bad cartographers.
The sense of essence, incense, et cetera
turns to mascara, as a gyre turns.
The island in the ocean, the bull's

Invention, the kingdom of Africa's too small!
We'll find our way, wrong, lost & tall.
Rome, the poet, after all
leads a syllable by a thread, & the conundrum is lethal.

## TARZAN'S TESTAMENT

### After Villon

I shiver all aflame, naked as a worm.
Hot as fire, I die of thirst beside a fountain.
Jane! Jane! I laugh through tears & wait without hope.
Well-received, I rejoice and have no pleasure.
I am strong, but have neither force nor power.
In my own country I live in a far-off land.
*My only comfort lies in sad despair.*

Yet richly dressed in furs, & trembling tooth on tooth,
I shiver, laugh, and wait without hope.
I await an inheritance and yet am no man's heir.
Jane! Jane! I win & yet remain the loser.
Who speaks the truth most tells me lies.
Nothing's more obscure than what's evident & certain.
When I lie down I have a great fear of falling.
My only comfort lies in great despair.

### 2.

Jane! Jane! go take a bath!
*And when you're there take off your clothes & use the tub.*

I'm never careful but I make all the efforts.
The black crow is nothing but a white swan on a flying trapeze.

## BRAILLE

I march for you Nancy, I march for you, Hugh
mama! papa! city! Vita! I march for you, too
I wrote a poem, still toying with the labyrinth
At the end of the line, Larry Rivers was painting a sign
I march for Hunter. I do not march for Kennedy, the KKK
the unions, the universities, the universe, the Rat Pack
jet set, *et al.*, the advanced middle-class, advancing
black or white, or the landlords, or spoiled
delinquents (distress signal: "May Day") or Stalin's ghost
That's all right. Peace! jobs! freedom! guns! George!
Georgia! I march where my footsteps tell. Like Gulliver
& millions, I've lived in the crack in the Liberty Bell
I march not for Meany, but more more, indivisible
Justice! Law! The sonnet is a form, the idiom indistinguishable.

## THE TUNNEL OF MIRRORS AT VERSAILLES

Speak to me not of movies, or love's reforms
The tangled bodies weave "coitus" "Laocoon"
I could not love you less, even, I'll love you more
(Once upon). Anxiety is negative triple time

*

Basie plays & sings at Snow's Ballroom, uptown, Nineteen Thirty Seven
& the rabble marches off to Quebec. In memory of George Washington.

# BIRTHDAY

## 1. HAVANA, 1928

To Irving & Gail

The century veering like a sparrow, seagull, hawk.
Famous female jukeboxes, galleons, elephants, with cocks
the size of men. Abortion time, or the negative of revolution.
Place, & characters. White veils are black & vice-versa,
whales, wheels in the darkness of the church; hospitals
ineluctably white. Girls, all classes, & fires in every
hotel. His head & beard shaved, in a clean suit, new shoes
& tie, going to Guatemala, my father rides a donkey.
At dawn he started from one or another European city,
& will never make the other shore or lighthouse. Could he,
if he wanted, I want to know, have looked back
& tasted salt? In the Barcelona of the future
he'll publish texts in 30 languages more terrible
than St. John of the Cross. & my mother, tho I'll never
do her justice, will undo one mistake & learn to sew.
On the beach, near the reach of water, I'm born, I think,
scream, conscious when I lie or dream or speak the truth, & able
to say, "Me", "You", "Here", "Time", "Place", "Remember",
"Fight", "Live", "Accept", "Love", "Death", "Fuck", "Hate".

## 2. COVENANT

To Michael O'Brien

China, characteristic, characteristically intact
at least, that is, the space of a line & theme of the whole
In & out of time two governments manage to thrive
"History," the rabbi said, "is the tool of survival"

Two nuns clippity-clap down the stairs
like film, one is Raggedy Ann, the other a doll
The street is Switzerland, cobbled Istanbul, Leningrad
Disneyland, sweating out the battle of ideas, & struggle for Man's soul

To be a Jew is to wear one's undershirt inside out
have two haircuts, one Yiddish, the other eternal
The choo-choo clock traverses the dimensions, rails
lines, daughters named Jessica & Rachel, a son Mihail

The cock of time is indeed Platonic. The schoolbells
ring in schools, the world, figures
magic carpets kings embroidered, lyrics in it, themselves & stars
Peacocks are crowing mute discs, nightingales, a sense of dramatics

Matzos in Cracow recalls the season's barking, & ghetto's cataclysm
The false Messiah's come & gone, over the river, over the border
waiting for Lefty, potatoes & theses all the time
The author died. His son-in-law sells boots to an English girl

working out of ------------'s office in a Maryland secretarial pool
When Forrestal, like France, jumped out of the nuthouse window
he broke frames, took two generations of the world & power, like summer, with him

### 3. Postcard on the Run, March 16th

To Judy Bishop

Let them eat cheesecake, caricature, style. I take the bus ride.
This is the most European quarter of the city. The houses
along Riverside Drive are more beautiful than the Palisades.
The day is grey, not lovely, the taxis anonymous; stoned
finally with the reconstructed, compassionate Buddha. 105th St.

The essays write charades, on the way to the Bridge. A waiter
& a printer, a striker named George, educated & naturally
Intelligent, goes to Yeshiva, while in 1936–1963, the way
the ball bounces, the Prince of Wales, Fred Astaire
dances mathematics perpetually. I have known the songs

of others. The day is long.
The bride is being & character. The Prince of Wales will never
marry. The Minister of War is a call girl. Last night
I dreamed I asked Cary Grant if he was happy. The girls
flock like pigeons on cement, converted into women. How should

I complain, then, if Prosperity & the State have proved
disjunct, in a world of agents, & Spring is coming?

## 4. Unlettered Lament

To Hunter Ingalls

It's tough when you can't determine
who are men & who are women
My life, like a past sentence
reminiscent of an age of kings
I'm sure is fiction, my voice
at best, merely classical, like death
If I could have my day, & have my way
I'd probably murder everybody
just to demonstrate my feelings
which are, or were, real. Maybe
the typewriter is both an image & a tool
& if the abyss is the kiss' structure
I'd qualify Europe, sure, Dionysus, too
Like summer, refracted, a nest of mirrors.

## 5. Around the Island

To Edward Field

Adam & Eve in the zoo, in the ark
the day of naming of the animals stopped.
An aggrieved map & globe of pictures!

Action & scene perpetually suspended between two wars!
A mummy with a hearing aid, once a buccaneer,
grabs at a microphone attached to a tiger by the tail,

announces, says, "Comrades,
The monsters at the world's end are real,
umbilical, two-dimensional, & setting sail."

6.

going to Spain, going to prison in sunshine
labyrinth outside
all the photographs are of birds without hands
The image has been transposed, redefined
it hurts, but happiness can only happen a year at a time.

Should a poem have a title?

From the double meaning of the word Cael, which signifies "strangers", as well as Gauls or Celts, some have imagined that the ancestors of the Caledonians were of a different race from the rest of the Britons, and that they received their name upon that account. This opinion, they say, is supported by Tacitus, who, from several circumstances, concluded that the Caledonians were of German extraction. A discussion of a point so intricate, at this distance of time, could neither be satisfactory nor important.

"Three days feasted the kings: on the fourth their white sails arose. The winds from the north drove Fingal to Morven's woody land. But the spirit of Loda sat in his cloud behind the ships of Frothal. He hung forward with all his blasts, and spread the white-bosomed sails. The wounds of his form were not forgotten! he still feared the hand of the king!"

## POEM

The image on the water is either a moon or a half-moon.
(The image is a river.)
It is perceived either by a girl playing a lute
Or a poet thinking of a crane.

The crane is not an image, nor any bird.
The poet is not an image, nor the river,
Or girl, or lute. The water is not an image. In fact,
There is no such thing as an image, except maybe the moon.

If he is drunk, Michael Drayton will resolve us.
His accent betrays the moon & its images.
We drink little but manage to see just as deep.
On the swing, the moon is cupped in the arms of Nature, dust rising.

# PORTRAIT OF A LADY

I.

Eyes like ellipses, described as pools,
at once the ocean, altho
not aquamarine, & a pair of almond seeds
pear-shaped, like crabs, wherein
moontides tied as to the strings of an apron,
tugged gently, flourished & played,
all urgency in the beholder's guise,
clarity only in the depths of the maid,
tho, here, perhaps my reading falters
& memory fades. A knowledgeable traveller,
once a connoisseur, landlocked
again after seven years, told me he was told
in Rio Espedras that eyes & the dance
are considered there organs & agents of love.
He spoke again & again of Sophia's shoulders,
& told me a story how once after a ball
in the late nineteenth century she began filling
Nature's abhorred vacuum. The slightest,
gangrenous incipiency, it, all in all,
came to nought. "Ideas like figures
& parasoled notes accompanied the waves
touching the silver beach. They
waltzed & waltzed & waltzed themselves dizzy.
Oars like knives dipped, dipped like blades."
I listened, softened. She knew no other shell or birth,
or softer procrustacean bed,
"no other shell, or berth, or softer, procrustacean bed."

## 2. Arachne

*Furioso.* The days Arachne weaves
intent upon their ways like planets in their skies
on her strung loom, streadin' & abobbin'
a solipsist's pattern
no stronger & no larger than the Brooklyn Bridge
(the Spider reviewed his Masterwork)
These days went on
till Zeus like thunder appeared, commanded Arachne
but she wouldn't obey
& list to a tune of veils, as Salome would
another day. She said, "See
I've woven myself this gown. It's white
seamless, a garden of the flesh
Here I've stayed, a Penelope, doing & undoing
I'll rest upon my handiwork."
Zeus
confounded, nonplussed, confused
cuckolded without a bed
no creature's form to turn into
turned Arachne instead
O Spider! spider
tempered, a distant star, I watch, see & witness
wiles
unicorns married, merry, umbilical
& sporting, chaste, where your catastrophe should be!

## THE POEM ON THE WALL

In 810 A.D. Yuan Chen wrote his friend the poet Po Chu-i
that on his way to exile he found one of his poems inscribed
on the walls of the Lo-k'ou Inn.


    The clumsy poem I wrote on the wall
no one much cared to see.
    Birdshit & moss' growth obscured it,
    Letters & all. An exile came, a page
to the throne, travelling. He didn't
    mind using his fancy sleeve to wipe
    the dirt away so he could read.

summer. I served time
I tried to unbend. I tried
to sew the figleaf back on

autumn. I dedicated the moon.
I saw it blossom like a de-
generate calf. I tried to laugh

spring. I went walking
I went to the movies, anticipating.
I tried to keep warm.

winter. I prayed to the sun.
I prayed to the moon.
I tried to keep warm.

PRAXIS

Like certain streets are troubadours,
To the bureaucrat flight is space.
The image of flight is power.

Politics relates images to the world.
I remembered the dream while shaving.
Like Hegel & Marx, I stood on my head.

The darkness remembers the flowers,
The beautiful white flowers
After the gate to the pasture has withered.

# HOMAGE TO A. CONCEIVED OF AS A SONG

This room is a prison.
I eat candy bars.
I read *Paris-Soir*,

smoke cigarettes.
I won't work.
The sun is gold bars.

I double you, double you,
like bear-dancing hours,
& wildernesses

up in honey & smoke.
I eat cigarettes,
newspaper tars.

My hair is gold braid
tho my soul may be black.
The image imagines

a red cigarette.
The rest is distraction,
art for the art.

I read newspaper skyscrapers
from the caged heart.

## NEWS

Though Helen's breasts were cups
we drank from troughs,
failing to invent the world's economy.

We wrap fish,
search out Cleopatra's needle in a haystack.
("Latin & grain are sacred," Ezra Pound said.)

I waited. Genet kissed me.
The world left a mousetrap at the door.

An old man tamed by time
  An old man on the grass with a lass
  An old man turned by time

Buttocks reading Ovid, turning the page
  Like a leaf of grass, not to avoid the turning
  The time, the turn, 10 o'clock falling

& the poem to be written, not in Los Angeles or such
  The highway meridian turns to dust, blooming like a cactus
  Or a line by Ovid, well-written this Spring

O love, I must!
  The turning in time toward the Atlantic's August
  Like money, confidence, thrusts the thigh's song

# GENESIS

## 1. ODE TO THE APOLLO

The view from the squadcar: Come Back,
Africa & Black Orpheus is a possible
double-feature, but the show goes on,
cowboys & spaceships, Tom Mix,
Dick Tracy & the pilot-watch, like
rat tat tat tick tock forever on the
anvil of the heart; & gorge rises
to submarine pressure, geysers, spumes,
white kittens & mice, as Count Basie
plays. The brass chorus is voice, always;
Charlie Christian clown-romances, two-steps,
boxes, waltzes Capt. Bligh. In the dark
Fats Waller plays prepossessed organs,
imaginary operas treading dialogues. Sammy
Davis lives! Like a cruel half-brother,
Hercules, the second hero frees Prometheus,
as Abraham imitating Moses comes down
the mountain side. Stardust! come eleven!
Backdrops like sweatshops, stagelights
imitate the absence of summer. Foolish
Woolworth's goes on strike.
The crime was ever universal. Buck!
Bubbles! Lead kindly, lights.

## 2. MODERN MUSEUM

Death by taxi-riding. Flee
the diagonal huntress, Diane-moon
multicolored through the revolving glass
where everyday angels and voyeurs trespass.
The Garden is checkered green.
Statues & supports supplant the Queen.
The sun blinds me.
Under palms I sweat, smoking wrung irony.
Alice-among the-Guernicas harangues
the mobiles and giants. The statues right
charades. In the Cave, Charlie plays,
Fairbanks leaps, the silver screen parades
alive, in person.
Greta leads Edna into visible Eden.
Devices flicker, the scene is won, written
on water. Poets count their seven schemes:
homburgs, bowlers, derbies, dowries, diaries,
sirens, us! Every bit is comedy and jazz,
borne on Sunday. A nude madonna
and child ascend the stair.
Where are the snows of yesteryear?

## 3. Picture

A checkerboard canvas, a black bull &
white horse, one two feet solid upon
the ground, keeping its victim receptive,
askew, interlocked in combat
& conquest: half their legs the gate-regular
strings of a lyre, there's gore
in red lines only. Bodiless heads,
cartoons practically, spectate
the amphitheatre, witness whisperlessness,
their own dumb alarm, Leda's body,
the body of the Swan. Host, population,
bald-headed, see: ivory in the slicker
delight of her teeth, her candy-striation
body, her upturned, poker-dotted hooves.
(Piano; piano). & from her hollow, mirror
belly, themselves spawned, black roosters,
black hens, equally, & white speculating hawks, that's all.

A LA CARTE

Littlenecks & cherrystones are cultured clams from Cape Cod.
The house is not a digestive apparatus.
What cannot be bought is the character of the specious.

What cannot be bought is the character of the *species*.
Littlenecks & cherrystones are cultured clams from Cape Cod.
Over Cape Cod, over Freeport & Port Washington

I wandered lonely as a cloud's digestive apparatus,
difficult as asparagus.

## THE DOG'S TALE

I chased my shadow, the chimera, across fields of print,
o then plains of film. The light was always red & green. I
went to Hoboken, smoked a cigar, & learned the rules of the
game. Object syllogism: flowers & nylon, anxious the bra,
cartoon-corsets of rhetoric. In the past there was a tree,
its ground & scale its own. "Enormous & handsome," its
syntax like expression, it seemed to make things grow. My
partners in the enterprise issued stock. We made a million,
pissed away a small fortune, tho even at this date I cannot
name the stroke. I long for Hoboken, whatever scene that was,
valentines & callgirls reading newspapers, coupled mannikins
like lorelei, color & rotation, wishing for the world.

## ONE MORE TIME

I'm gonna tell your ma
& tell your pa
& send you back to Arkansas

(I take that thing).
*Take your time.*
She can do the birdland all night long.

## GW. "THE WIND"

First he flung coin & cross across the Potomac,
then crossed the Rubicon at Trenton. Pockmarked,
of false teeth, who was heroic as a steeplejack,
he eschewed Eden, a paradise of cherry trees,
sense, hens: hence, Cardinal Noumenon, & "things Japanese".
Anyway, I've lived now & seen everything:
the scene as pastel-pastiche device,
Larry Mississippi's painting; icons, monuments,
post-kinema prose, the Grand Canyon, "like nothing"—
& a mannikin off 5th, taking the air,
a little round hole like death in her stocking.

## DEPOSITION

The highway was Nemesis. I did not take the freedom ride. On dirty afternoons her rooms were dirty thighs. Her high heels abandoned her brassiere. Her hair flew out the window. The clock between her lips smuggled incense & brine. I sang the marriage of ghosts & pornographers. Our universe was filled with dolls. We spoke French & English, mainly, & topics of correction. Not clocked, her stockings caught fish. Like a slow pitch the sun beat birdlike through the air. She had to go to work. I waited for her & I drowned.

## K's HYMN TO ZEUS IN MEMORY OF CLARK GABLE

By Thee the wide world & firmament of Heaven swings,
Is guided in its wheeling & dying round this Earth,
Yea, in bright, glad, happy submission, for in thy Hand
a mighty breed, Bird & Tree, the Thunderbolt is,
double-edged & wrought with never-ending Fire. Sir, Sire
the pulse of life that beats in all created things
Is thine & walks Thy way. The Omnipotent Word—the Kiss—
Thou dost direct & manipulate thru all Creation,
cartoons escaping illustration & mingling with the Sun
& Company of stars is ours, whose Time & senile, mobile
Nation makes thee Great King, all that is, & names thee God.

## LOOKING FOR GIORGIONE

A chorus of women dreaming a season, a line like a wreath.
  The ghost poem travels on the merry-go-round, green as money
Or a note by Mallarmé.
  The hunter's poem fells the leopard, square as a diamond. She
made reality out of flowers, Hamlet's daughter. The bird is a word
named Robespierre. The scenes are like flowers. The weeds
  are like flowers & nothing's withered. The ocean's
  In the wind, & the parasols are enlightened. Beautiful
glass rests on the small crown of her head.
  It's my vanity that has me believe there are no physical
dimensions. Threatened,
  Like a psychological nosegay, the circle of snow was rendered invisible.
We carried the torah, blowing the bagpipe tune, like World War I, over NY city rooftops.

## CONVERSATIONS

They made the world & missed reality
the crude nude, the usual paradox
the landscape scenery of the mind, epic as a figleaf, is a globe

By windows Landowska plays Bach, the Yasnaya Polyana estates
the mermaid by the window listens, anchored to the spot
the idols of the living room are smashed, digested calendars

Milkcrates, water, weeds, aeroplanes, news of revolution, too
that just happen to happen, Atlantis' ghetto garland & fuse
Nouns dance like lollipops, & the sun is high & dark

At Heaven's gate there are pearl-handled revolvers & green hatchecks
the roller-skating kids draw beads on God's face
the adjectives are willing, but the spirit of the place isn't great

In August or September the lady in red washes down a vodka cola
the tortoise shell comb climbs like a flame at Aristotle's behest
& the world spins on its axis, Stalingrad, orbiting the earth

The moon's cock transcends George Washington Bridge
Newport is missing. The Alaskan Earthquake regurgitates, regulates
a lost continent. In Atlantic City beetles & mermaids sing

Lost in the Cow Palace, as lost in NY
the devil is a special black pearl & plays the fiddle, left-handed
the figleaf is green as a giant's beard, tho the desert's unwilling

There is no such thing as a witch. Just broomsticks, & the world is great
of a poetic order, filled with marches. The swamps invade the castle gates
The harpsichords like wooden Indians throw cigar boxes at the fireworks

& who can remember to survive survives. A leaf falls
multiplying time's tomb. For a second, the underworld
was visible. Praise what was ordered a second in the mind

# THE VEGETABLE CALENDAR

& they become tigers in daytime, the five thumbs of existentialism
Like a kid falling off his bike in September, on his way to school. &
the last leaf in the wind turns at Land's End, simulating seashells
& mother of pearl. & Titans' trumpets herald dusk, like dawn. Scales
are registered now at Eton, & Aaron, like a pen, via television, is the
football game in the living room, the verisimilitude of the pineapple
the Lamb & middle-class. It's raining cats, dogs, sharks, arks, syllables
& pin-stripe suits, & what's known is forgotten every day of the week
The calendar trips a kid, a Lucky Strike merchant selling us a war
& Victory, shorthand for the misbegotten, burns like a phoenix. No matter
Atlantis, any regurgitated, resurrected myth. News will speak like law
The right mistake, it's not too much to ask! It is. Weeks are wise as
witches, broomsticks are true stomachs & beget mermaids. Galley slaves
work like wristwatches at the wrong turn, the right detour. Songs thru
the labyrinth spell the path thru Panama. Entrism. Niagara. Phrenology
of the Northwest Passage. Cannibalism, a code of war. Armed with
a pick-axe, I stitched skulls, sought rare cactus, a continent below
the belt. However, the season was wrong. It began at Vichy. I was talking
to Prez, swallowing water, & travelling to a war. I counterfeited huge
sums for the sake of a cause, for the sake of the music, all of which
was lost with all the newsreel footage the League of Nations had.
Trains took me everywhere & nowhere, then planes, & sewing machines
yes, a needle travelling backwards, ass backwards, spinning to the eye

## JUNKIE IN PARADISE

When I was young & glad, neurotic & miserly & photographed easily
I believed
without knowing it, that if I wrote a poem that was beautiful
& was worthy, I'd become a millionaire
& everyone in the world would be happy
Christ! I could walk to the moon & invent printing again!
But I worried & went to Spain, Spain beautiful as an earring
& yes life taught me otherwise to twist the neck of real ambition
& Daddy Rorschach ministered me thumbnail sketches
I saw mousetraps beautiful as earrings     pamphlet sunsets over
the Grand Canyon     the West Side.     hitchhikers at dawn     strange fish
Both ways     Estates.     blond swimming pools.     Forget-me-nots
& the man who invented the xylophone self-endowed with chuckles & a checkbook
& the cinematographer ought to be smart enough not to bust more than one nut at a time
He is / half the faun    .     Angles
He is
& altho it may be too late to be said right in this place
let it be said, nevertheless & broadcast frequently
Our time is a history of derangement. & Birthday Parties
& who prints my poems is printing money, truly
The purse in enormous
& counterfeit. In the light of everything
In the wind
straws to build the pyramids. Straws to break the camel's back

# TRANSLATIONS

We put thirty spokes together and call it a wheel;
But it is on the space where there is nothing that the utility of the wheel depends.
We turn clay to make a vessel;
But it is on the space where there is nothing that the utility of the vessel depends.
We pierce doors & windows to make a house;
& it is on these spaces where there is nothing that the utility of the house depends.
Therefore, just as we should take advantage of what is,
We should recognize the utility of what is not.


### 2.

In highest antiquity people did not know private property.
Later on families acquired it & held it in high repute.
Still later this led to fear & reviling.
Truly, it is not by trusting people that mistrust is generated.
How remote from this were the sages, brief of speech!
For when their tasks were accomplished, their work done,
Throughout the country everyone said, "It all came to us quite naturally."


### 3.

Thirty spokes combine to make a wheel.
When there was no private property carts were made for use.
Clay is formed to make vessels.
When there was no private property vessels were made for use.
Windows & doors go to make a house.
When there was no private property houses were made for use.
Thus, private property leads to profits for the feudal lords,
But not having it leads to use for the people.

TIME

Q. What is Suzy Parker doing on the cover of *Fortune*?
A. Getting older.

Q. Why is there only one Eiffel Tower?
A. Because it eats its young.

*

Anthropologically, Mexico doesn't exist.

*

Perhaps it is better to read the book as fiction. Hemingway recommends just that in an introduction where he says, ironically, that it "may throw some light on what has been written as fact." Take his account of F. Scott Fitzgerald. The indictment by anecdote is irresistibly funny, but was the author of *The Great Gatsby* such a petulant clown, fatuous snob, & pathetic simpleton about sex? Or Hemingway's saying Zelda Fitzgerald almost destroyed Scott through her insane envy of his talent by convincing him he was sexually inadequate. Hemingway claims that he realized she was insane long before Fitzgerald was forced to accept the fact. As evidence, he cites the time Zelda asked him: "Don't you think Al Jolson is greater than Jesus?" Perhaps the lost generation was not really lost after all, merely mislaid.

*

He knew this well enough himself. In one anecdote he brilliantly recreates a scene at the Dome Café, where the doomed painter Pascin is drinking with 2 model-tarts or tart-models. "He grinned with his hat on the back of his head. He looked more like a Broadway character of the '90s than the lovely painter he was, & afterwards, when he had hanged himself, I liked to think of him as he was that night at the Dome. They say the seeds of what we do are in all of us, but it always seemed to me that in those who make jokes in life the seeds are covered with better soil & with a higher grade of manure." *Is this a man writing the obituary of another man or his own?*

*

His own. The other man.

# EL DORADO

(On Seeing a Picture of Jonas Mekas in *The Village Voice*)

Sure he's crazy just like me, & fill the jails with unjust laws
The dirty movie we saw in high school stayed in our repertoire
Predicted to go far, we went nowhere
eating candy & film clips
Made a movie or two on a shoestring, thinking of vaudeville
& every possible pratfall legislated underground, like clowns
& mushrooms, & the bazooms of movie stars, every machine

But the money kept coming in from Moscow, never stopped
Like perverse children we determined to turn back the clock
before it annihilated Jack Smith & others
& the presses were kept warm should it be necessary to print cash
or a book of drawings of butterflies & flowers, & beagles, harmless creatures
St. Francis tripped over on his first zoological expedition, travelling
post-war, like a mendicant Italian movie company looking for an American market

We didn't elect a president, but named him Orpheus. He might have been named Auden
Any appeal to conscience might mean a bullet-ridden sarcophagus
today, now, in this city & state, NY, brother
Naturally, the Mafia can be counted upon & will do its part
A new line of jokes will issue from the jailhouse, imbedded with blues & laws
&, Easter winging in, at least one masterpiece entitled "Resurrection Symphony"
Bureaucracy is Nature, our lives the landlords' flock of rats & dogs

Only Niggers are free to murder their ghosts, & marry Hamlet's father
Who had our mouths washed out with televised toothpaste & saved our eyes
We'll flock like a chorus, like birds, & name all the children we love

# THE MACHINERY OF PARADISE

paradox. Noise. Let Paradise be set up in a somewhat lofty place;
let there be put about it curtains & silken hangings, at such
an height that those persons who shall be in Paradise can be seen
from the shoulders upward; let there be planted sweet-smelling
flowers, & foliage; divers trees therein, & fruits hanging upon
them, so that it may seem a most delectable place. Then let the
Saviour come, clothed in a dalmatic, & let Adam & Eve be set before
him, Adam clothed in a red tunic, & Eve in a woman's garment of white,
& a white, silken wimple. & let both of them stand before the
Figure of God, but Adam a little nearer with a composed countenance,
& Eve with a countenance a little more subdued. & let Adam be
instructed when he shall make his answers, lest in answering he be
either too fast or too slow. Let not only Adam but all persons be so
instructed that they shall speak composedly & shall use such gestures
as become the matter whereof they speak; & in uttering verses,
let them neither add a syllable nor take away, but pronounce all
clearly; & let those things that are to be said be said in their due
order. Whoever shall speak the name of Paradise, let him look back
at it & point it out with his hand. Then the Serpent, cunningly put
together, shall ascend the trunk of the forbidden Tree, unto which
Eve shall approach her ear, as if hearkening to counsel. Thereafter,
Eve shall take the apple, & offer it to Adam. Then shall Adam eat
a part of the apple, & straightway take knowledge of his sin; & he
shall bow himself down, so that he cannot be seen of the people, &
shall put off his goodly garments, & shall put on poor garments of fig-
leaves sewn together; &, exceeding great sorrow, shall begin his
lamentation. & after the fall of man, Adam & Eve shall be outside
of Paradise. Sad & confounded, they shall bow themselves to the ground.

## CHORUSES

The poem was beautiful.
Was the poem beautiful, or was the rain beautiful?
The rain was beautiful.
Was the rain beautiful, or was the room beautiful?
The room was beautiful.
The girl was beautiful. The music was beautiful.

The poem was beautiful. Was the poem beautiful, or was the rain
beautiful? The rain was beautiful. Was the rain beautiful, or was
the room beautiful? The room was beautiful.
The girl was beautiful. The music was beautiful. Music,
rain, room & poem. Beautiful.

The poem was beautiful. Beautiful.
The rain was beautiful. Beautiful.
The girl was beautiful. Beautiful.
The music was beautiful. Beautiful.
Music, rain, room, poem & girl.
Beautiful.

Was the poem beautiful, or was the rain beautiful?
The rain was beautiful. The poem was beautiful.
Was the rain beautiful, or was the room beautiful?
The room was beautiful.
Was the room beautiful, or was the girl beautiful?
The girl was beautiful. The rain was beautiful.
The room was beautiful.

The poem was beautiful.
Music, rain, room, girl & poem. Beautiful.

## POEM FOR RACHEL BLAU
## AFTER HER READING AT THE EVENTORIUM

### 1.

You break a path & find a river
each stone a muscle
Each step's a stone
& making it is getting there, song.

*

The typewriter is an image that can speak of sofas
The river can be caged like a bird
& as easily as wings break the wind's brake
Muscles & stones can be songs

*

The butterfly on the tennis court must be spiked
The badminton game continues singing "Lohengrin"

### 2.

I guess most ambitions are second rate, unless
that is, they're the real thing
Like a whale, the path of commitment; the moon
The moustache near the trombone

### 3.

Making it is getting there, song
The same river runs thru six centuries
The moon knits Ajax's wheel, the button on the coat
of the highwayman

### 4.

After the moving came the rain.
The gendarmes at the door spoke a foreign tongue.
Chinese anti-syllables greeted us as we sailed down the dawn.
We slid down the stairs

& quoted Chinese anti-syllables as soon as we saw the sun.
After the rain came the moving. Then the dawn.
The foreign tongue spoken by the gendarmes at the door was Chinese.
It sounded like a poem.

# INTRODUCTIONS

"Mary McCarthy, meet Susan Sontag. Susan Sontag, meet Mary McCarthy."
"F. Scott Fitzgerald, meet John Keats. John Keats, meet F. Scott Fitzgerald."
"Arthur Cohen, meet Hunter Ingalls. Hunter Ingalls, meet Arthur Cohen."
"Joe DiMaggio, meet Marilyn Monroe. Marilyn Monroe, meet Joe DiMaggio."
"Norman Mailer, meet Norman Weisselberg. Norman Weisselberg, meet Norman Mailer."
"Howard Everngam, meet Howard Nemerov. Howard Nemerov, meet Howard Everngam."
"Irving Howe, meet Max Shachtman. Max Shachtman, meet Irving Howe."
"Linda Lev, meet Leonard Lipton. Leonard Lipton, meet Linda Lev."
"Judith Malina, meet Antonin Artaud. Antonin Artaud, meet Judith Malina."
"Lionel Trilling, meet Choo-Choo Johnston. Choo-Choo Johnston, meet Lionel Trilling."
"Mark Stern, meet Irving Feldman. Irving Feldman, meet Mark Stern."
"Northrop Frye, meet Wm. Shakespeare. Wm. Shakespeare, meet Northrop Frye."
"Ernest Hemingway, meet Ernest Truex. Ernest Truex, meet Ernest Hemingway."
"Lana Turner, meet Larry Rivers. Larry Rivers, meet Lana Turner."
"Linda Darnell, meet Jackie Wilson. Jackie Wilson, meet Linda Darnell."
"Kenneth Anger, meet Jonas Mekas. Jonas Mekas, meet Kenneth Anger."
"Karl Bissinger, meet Diane Arbus. Diane Arbus, meet Karl Bissinger."
"Elizabeth Taylor, meet Elizabeth Montgomery. Elizabeth Montgomery, meet Elizabeth Taylor."
"Herb Bronstein, meet Harold Rosenberg. Harold Rosenberg, meet Herb Bronstein."
"Dov Lederberg, meet Jimmy Hoffa. Jimmy Hoffa, meet Dov Lederberg."
"Al Capp, meet Huntington Hartford. Huntington Hartford, meet Al Capp."
"Michael Benedikt, meet Michael Smith. Michael Smith, meet Michael Benedikt."
"Cassius Clay, meet Captain Steve. Captain Steve, meet Cassius Clay."
"Allen Arbus, meet Andy Warhol. Andy Warhol, meet Allen Arbus."
"Leon Trotsky, meet Jean Cocteau. Jean Cocteau, meet Leon Trotsky."
"Sholem Aleichem, meet Mark Twain. Mark Twain, meet Sholem Aleichem."
"Fred Astaire, meet Arthur Murray. Arthur Murray, meet Fred Astaire."
"Rachel Carson, meet Capt. Cousteau. Capt. Cousteau, meet Rachel Carson."
"Laurel & Hardy, meet Mutt & Jeff. Mutt & Jeff, meet Laurel & Hardy."
"Dame Rumor, meet Damon Runyon. Damon Runyon, meet Dame Rumor."
"Miss America, meet Miss Universe. Miss Universe, meet Miss America."
"Aaron Cohen, meet Bela Kun. Bela Kun, meet Aaron Cohen."
"Omer Simeon, meet Colin Young. Colin Young, meet Omer Simeon."
"Marshall McLuhan, meet Harvey Matusow. Harvey Matusow, meet Marshall McLuhan."
"Walt Whitman, meet Henri Rousseau. Henri Rousseau, meet Walt Whitman."
"George Kennan, meet Genghis Khan. Genghis Khan, meet George Kennan."
"Captain Video, meet Captain Kangaroo. Captain Kangaroo, meet Captain Video."

# PARADISE NEWS

The ideal chick flies up the stairs
I held on to summer as if it were a flag

What do they want?
Your mother & World War II

A siren
An image of China sounded in my mind like a gong

Paradise ladies walk in 3's & pairs
The ideal chick flies up the ideal stairs

The young cat was dead by an ashcan. He lost
his first fight. News is an image of Paradise

What do they want?
An image of China sounded in my mind like a flag

I held on to Everest as if it were a flag
The ideal chick flies up the ideal stairs

News is an image of Paradise, & it seems to me
as if that scream were still piercing my brain

Like your mother or World War II
news is an image of Paradise

& tragi-comedy a medium long close-up
The ideal chick flies up the stairs

The young cat was dead by the ashcan
having lost his first fight

The pigeons usually get away
She heard birds outside her window speaking Greek

I'm nothing if not critical
The ideal chick flies up the stairs

News is an image of Paradise
An image of China sounded in my mind like a gong

One image tells another, & it seems to me
I can still hear that scream piercing my brain

POEM

### Instructions for Making Movies

    Aim the camera up at the sky & shoot.
Load the camera with green leaves.
    Load the camera with orange leaves.
      Aim the camera at the face of the beloved.
      Attend all demonstrations, disguising the camera as arms or legs.
        Load the camera with pigeons & shoot.
          Think of the Italian Renaissance.
            Put it on tape. Take a walk.
              Put Griffith Park in the camera & shoot.
              Load the camera with Las Vegas & shoot.

### A Catalogue of Films

Black graphic (negative) light sleep shit core
chinese gong/substance brave typewriter tits lists
Flowers houses trees beards clean-shaven Birth
love news encyclopedia Blues rhythm roses
Chants chance collages changes Translations mirrors
vertebrae Facts lists ladders ascend toes
Mirrors news encyclopedias Goethe Vergil
Apollinaire james Farrell ships catalogues
warriors figure heads tribes Fires interviews
Memory/s mimeograph machines news Birds news

### Dirty Words

"Project" is a dirty word. "Relationship" is a dirty word.
"Little magazine" is a dirty word.
"Experimental film" is a dirty word.
"Montage" is a dirty word.
"Dialogue" is a dirty word. "Translation" is a dirty word.
"Enormous" & "fabulous", "Machinery" & "orthodox"
are dirty words. "Escalation" is a dirty word.
"Abraham" & "Straus" are dirty words.

# EPITHALAMIUM COMPOSED

Upon Hearing Henry Hudson Sing "*The September Song*"

1.
I'm a man of decision. I always flip a coin.
And the Morning Star huckalooed to the Ladies.
At first they fought tooth & nail
    But when it came to blows,
They who had the stronger lungs
    Blew off the other's nose.
    & we who plotted pyramids, diapers obtain.

2.
The other night I had a dream
    (I dream in circles just before dawn)
I swear I saw Hamlet's ghost
Marching up & down the lawn. A scenario was
    seen. I dreamed againe
    Four girls playing house constructed
    an American flag. They sang,

"We who plotted pyramids, diapers obtain."
Clouds marched by. & a pastoral hill
    stumbled. A pickpocket took out
    a harmonica, & with his other hand
Rolled himself a cigarette
    *Beau Geste*. (It became a watch.)
    And the Morning Star huckalooed to the Ladies.

3.
Was it not ever thus? I was lucky.
Lucky as Ulysses. I made several voyages
    & plotted pyramids. & huckalooed to the Ladies
    The stars in their courses were not men on horses
but ships of state, deserts. They
    Like Ulysses, huckalooed to the Ladies
    baited breath, & plotted pyramids, three hats.

4.
     "& we who diapers obtain, plotted pyramids." Again
     'Cause every nose is a rose
     & ev'ry Sea Venus has wings. Time is of the
Garden, summer on the wrist
     And every labyrinth a pyramid (of diapers),
     yes, three hats. Thru leaves
     The moon, at 3 o'clock, hangs like a suit of light.

## FROM AXE TO LENT

The cinema was never silent. From its beginnings it was necessary to put the ear asleep so the eye could hear. This was an aphorism, like the imported necessity of television. Wherever they went there was the same list of chains. All the classics were snipped into fragments. In an obscure detachment. How's that? Tom Sawyer wanted to know. Sound cinema was born.

Then technical discoveries removed the necessity of abandoning musical montages to the moribund fancy of orchestra leaders, & permitted them, the *lieder*, to be definitively inscribed on the edge of the film. None of which, as Tom Sawyer well knew, would stop the fucking anarchists from throwing bon-bons.

The wind cascaded thru the window pane.

*Gnus-of-the-World*. "Guns of the Trees".

Autumn Leaves. September Songe.

But the same aberrations continue. Every day bears witness: indecent spectacles . . . artistic violations, a few francs. Infamous salads.

"What?" said Lenin, "is to be done?" "Your movie, copper," said the chess game, upside down. I used to try to wash it off with water. Piecemeal. The classics. Prunes like water, heavy & blue. Paillasse. The snows of Westchester, yesteryear. Where?

I continued to write. Never a letter. Never a sentence. Never a phrase. Never a note.

Muscles. Icicles. *Mise-en-scenes*.

Songs.

They never sang.

MOON

These days my lunar moon isn't phased.
Cycles occupy the sun
& Ruth Adams rides a milk train
to the Luxembourg Gardens.
On the beach, near the reach of water
a dog trots. Paradise
is circumstantial, like irons in the
fire; loss. A brief case, up in arms.
Wooden heels. Weal of metaphors.
& a staircase.

2.

The volume is a whale & cannibal
a single dimension in the face of time. Mistaken
Two brothers struggle at an angle, spell
the death of things
Legs. Infinite legs
*do the twist like we did last summer.*
Music travels thru the waves of her hair.
She witnesses despair at the seashore.
water. Resurrection. Metaphysics. Flesh
For her mathematics & mumbo-jumbo
are the same syllabus.

3.

Play is criticism. There is
an image of whiteness. Seashells.
There is an image of asparagus. Kiosks. Letters.
*the withness of the body*; words, translation, & corrupted dance
That's all there is, folks
Travelling to mind
the book
like the body, is no problem.

4.

Amen. An imaginary violin, walking
amen. Handcuffs
Once upon a time.

# REMEMBRANCE OF THINGS ROCK & ROLL

The way of the wind they blow too
  weatherstruck & vain. A cracked number of voices
    names their song. Their metier
      ghost beliefs & shaggy-dog sentences
        any wonder then we're preparing for war?

      Call me if you wish Arete the ape of my own confession
        or, mist-like desire's ghost & echo
            bitter fruit in a woman's ear.
            Kings wear their seal & crown of sovereignty

            In one eye. I needed real clothes.
            But most of all I needed not to die. Pigs, I know
sport & swim in the mud of sties like swans. But Athene
the Goddess made me, made me wholly strong & wise, tho she
            too believes a mind should solve its riddles
            of conscience, make of them stratagems to outwit

            Circe, devices like the wooden horse.
            Ah, women! I know what I am, a bush set sailing
          its blade-like gleam perpetually mirroring an image
              of the sun. I'm naked! Naked! I'll row to Ithaca
                & strike! & see them run!

      2.
      Grant them the Paradise of their desire. Make them
      citizens of here & now & forever
          again.
          Watch them. As the day turns
          the world spins.
          Rotund. Rotund

AMERICAN *Journal* (for J.H.)


I've got news
Mama's got the blues
                    huge shadows
                    music, here & now
                                        occupies space

                    Proportions
                    dimensions, syllabus
                    A garden
                            of cliches  .  "Madness lies"
                            Heaven can wait

The shadow of the tree
casts a pillow on the ground. A terrace
                                    of shadows
                                    If you please  .  An Orient

                    in the shrubbery, rabbits
                    scarecrows. Like a tophat
                    the moon on the loose, lakes
every day.
Tunes are like shadows       .      On Tuesdays

                    or the hide-go-seek game of noise. The airplane flies
                    the machine stutters
                    bees in air-conditioners

Mama plays with dolls & pillows.
The violin
escapes the coffin. Huge shadows
                    spark, do not spark; spark & do not spark
                    the calligraphy of the dark.

                        Forty lines write a poem, the last resort
                                    of patriots. Twice
                                    if by day

# THE ENORMOUS CHORUS

& nobody alive knows no more what love is supposed to mean
because poets are engineers of the soul who build machines
for living; & anthology succeeds anthology as the night the
night; & the Cockney movie had no subtitles; & the banana
cake was delivered with tea leaves in it, reminiscent of tong
wars, from New Jersey, baked by a chicken-sexer; & still
they tell me, "Say 'Garden State'", & I say, "Garden State";
& the Princeton tiger came like Christ the kite, in September;
& TS Eliot read his poetry to a packed house; I mean audi-
torium; & the best modern furniture is designed by architects;
& Jack Smith is gonna die of happiness; & there'll be peace
in Viet Nam & we'll all be beautiful again (the typewriter
will write a poem entitled "Manufacture", or "War & Peace"
just for the poet & his friend); & the coin will stop spinning
& all the plays will be witty & largely beautiful; actresses
will acquiesce in their diction; & the gangster movie will be
produced, shot on location in Kansas, directed by a Frenchman;
the 'new wave' will roll to a dead halt on a black & white
highway; successful tycoons will burn all their paintings,
like nihilists, or Rouault, each in his Golden Pavilion; & the
lunch waiters will run the country, having taken over the news-
papers; & Grace Kelly & Robt. Kelly will tour paradise & Heaven,
remark Billie Holiday teaching Robt. Young how to play Daddy
& the saxophone; & Michelet will give us a worthy cosmology;
& the FBI will invent a twittering machine that works; &
there goes Richie Schmidt all dressed up, looking like a priest

# THE APPLES & THE PEACHES

I was walking along minding my own business
when this chicken New Deal appeared before
my very eyes. "How goes it, old bean," the chicken
New Deal inquired. "Just terrific," I replied.


2.

When I was young & in my prime, & didn't have
    a dime, was it a crime
      Studs Lonigan shaking peaches off the apple tree

Swinging like Cymbeline through Eden, I saw
    as I live & breathe the embrace of Hamlet &
      Henri IV (part I). & there was Lenin,
muttering, "What is to be done?"


3.

    Insure your future. Ask Emile Capouya.
& the announcement came embroidered with the stars & stripes
of Israel.
    "Chicken New Deal, chicken New Deal, chicken New Deal,"

    sang the lark.

## THE SPOTTED DOG

The true heroes of our city are the firemen.
  They're the true pagans, & enough to make me forget
    Crime, graft & corruption. They're song's music, &
      I love their engines. & because of them, I'll never
        Forget what it means to be a Red, & I'll never go
          To San Francisco, where the fairies are all athletes,
            & Poseidon's Waterfront Restaurant is owned by Joe DiMaggio.
        I don't care if the editor lives in Athens!
If only the junkies here would get some rest, stop stealing
  My furniture & television set, & would steal my poems instead!
    Then I'd make it my business to steal fire, as seriously
      As any workaday magpie. I'd get hold of Rousseau's music, known to exist,
        But only after having dressed him up as a fireman, pretty & serious
          As any of Rilke's dolls. If you don't believe me, ask
            Apollinaire. What an "Ode to the Fire Department" our chorus
        Could write! & don't think I don't long to get started. &
          don't think burning Xmas trees in January will ever satisfy me.

BABY

(after a passage by Lao-Tse)

I guess it's time we stopped kidding ourselves about books & words
& brainchildren. It's just no good, these fancy problems, & plain silly,
to boot. & misguided to think one thing leads to another. Tho
conventional types have a more or less easy time of it, make likely
pilgrimages, like church on Sunday, perpetual Christmas in their minds,
green trees always blooming, I'm just a local idiot, a fifth wheel,
& idle besides. A waif in disguise, not big enough to lift a finger.
These characters I know have something going everywhere, chips on every
number & square. I must be a joke not playing the game, having
already gone for broke & lost, once upon a time. Why, I couldn't get
to Delancey Street by myself if I tried! & I can't figure out the angles.
Another mistake! & I'm cool about it too, as if I were confident,
which I am. The lonely crowd's organized, seems to be making it, or
have it made, but I get nowhere, a fish out of water, & no roadmap;
pig-headed, awkward, "diff'rent", cooking an Empire with water & pot;
an infant, as a matter of fact, a little baby, still hot at the tit.

ego organization real estate money green bird green beard facts encyclopedias
mirrors money real estate narrative translation poetry press real estate
narrative ego hierarchy trees film fiction narrative poetry press real estate
news orange green blue organization real estate money images words poetry
narrative ego money black graphic negative light sleep shit house words facts
ego printing press camera typewriter tits lists flowers green bird green light
love birth news translations narrative vertebrae encyclopedias ladders facts
chants chance collages ascend toes feet typewriters leaves rhythm roses
fires green red yellow facts news encyclopedias essays news money Goethe Vergil
Apollinaire james Farrell ships catalogues microphones figureheads tribes
warriors fires interviews memories ships mimeograph machines news birds news

# TALISMAN

Fifteen
centuries
  ago
Ausonius
  walking
  in
  his
Italian
garden
  saw
  (he
says
so),
"All
my

Paestum
  roses
  laughing
  at
me."
He
immortalized
  them.
  Let
  them
  Grow,
an
anthology
  less
brass

than
  gold,
or
  getting
  warmer,
the
  shadow
of
  poetry,
or
  the
Swan's
  shadow,
a
  tableau.

## FEBRUARY 15TH

Is it February already? Irving, it's true
the middle voice is good, the psalm saves the cartoon, the outline
the very limitations of the graphic. The steel guitar, like an instrument of destiny

hangs on the side of the motorcycle, or on a tree, limb-like, a gypsy
The buildings of the city spin. They spin
in the rain, anchoring Atlantis again. There's nothing more to say
Fruit is knowledge

The parts of speech are the parts of the body
The role of the poet is poetry

MASQUE

"Child, ain't the Lexington Ave. bus just the slowest thing in this whole city?"

                              *

In 1923 Kafka went to Berlin.
"These steps lead to the Flick Theatre."
The road to hell is paved with cultivated gardens.
The world hangs by a thread of verbs & nouns.
The Greeks invented pain.
Gossip & anecdote were the first stories.
Morality is the imitation of an action.
Mythology is a disease of language.
Because it is there, I felt like spitting down.
The Ritz Bros. invented the telephone & airplane.
Ginger Rogers married Cyrano de Bergerac in 1641.
Dollie moving out, zoom moving in;
Mom dusts off first base, ump dusts off home plate. Choppers

BUFFALO

Newspapers, tabloid-size mirrors or bedsheet-size figleaves lie ritualistically
On the continent
Give me back my bike, my roller skates & red sled too
Give me back my *Beauty & the Beast*. I dare you
A slate-grey sky, a ghetto of Algerians in Paris
In Kansas rain turns dust to pearls, & Hemingway sleeps
with Marilyn Monroe. They dream together of bullfights
What occurs happens, parachutes like distribution.
The absurd is composed of the ridiculous. Paradox meets ambiguity
in the world. Roofs & towers echo vast distances, in fact, were
never known. Cherokees dance like maidens, except they move, blind, sown.

SIX

Figureheads of music are tattooed in the air as rock & roll rolls by in a conver-
tible car. In the city room news of China came in over the ticker tape. Foretold
 & then they sold the Bklyn Bridge to the Coliseum, American tourists
  Time is now the time of death; the history of love an anachronism, the history
   of crime irrelevant. The summer buzzards have arrived.
   Hand in hand they walked the streets of Pelham together, not each
   the image of the other. The braves are quiet again. The fires are going out.
   I await the glacial axe, resurrection, autumn. Once again a leaf falls

## POEM

My rediscovery of the sidewalk café is news.
I sit on a stoop in a neighborhood I lived in when I was a kid

in this city, not Hungary
in Hungary.

The summer is full of time.
I cannot get a drink

but drink, & drink.
(I sit on a stoop & wrote a song.)

## CHESS

The 3 kings who came to Havana in 1928
to attend my birth

I invented in NY, once upon a time.
Everyone knows "studio" means "love".

"Ripness is all." "Summer" means "full-time".
Indian summer is like an image of the eternal.

## POEM & VARIATIONS

Where are the snows of yesteryear?
Poor poets' sighs are heard afar
(He sleeps not, yet he snores)
& walks on feet that wear no shoes

& sings, like news
"I've got a right to sing the blues
I've got a right to hang around down by the river.
Who but my true love set this town on fire?"

I shall begin with a bunch of quite random remarks.
    "How do all the entr'actes get into the body politic?"
Everyone knows what's going on, poets carrying placards
    & writing plays
        Children marching, walking for peace on Easter Sunday
        cops everywhere, like artifacts of Nature;
Innocent people making dirty movies
        the trick being it's done without money, but on time & air
        & practically without cameras, or minds, for that matter
        If it's necessary for that to be said
        But that's why we're here. I look out the window,
a newspaper flies in my face & says, "It's August again,
    it's Spring, & everybody's going crazy & marching."

## CHINESE POEM

"Why, after nearly four years of comparative peace in that part of the world, did the Communists, without warning, begin to bombard the offshore islands in August 1958?"

*

Looking for jewels

The more the better
If we can't find them

In the earth
we'll go to the moon

# THE PASSIONATE POSTCARD

I know that two & two is five & it worries me.
Byron's father died when he was three.
(Your orbs are like moons, melons.)

"Very inspiring": the single glass of water
theory, Lilliputians, per se
tied down like Gulliver.
During the Depression, we tried, warily

To save soap, electricity
& the formula by Lenin. A tree grew in Bklyn.
The piano was born on a farm. In Harlem
Once upon a time.

The missing link is language.
I was common clay until roses were planted in me
Splash! The heroic couple pass thru the revolving door

# THE LIFE OF BIRD ORNSTEIN

Your postcards from Europe were
the high points of my summer.
They were my Alps & Pyrenees,
My Incas, Perus, & Paramount Pictures.

If I can spare the saliva &
salvage the sabotage,
I'll etch a feature, a tonsil, a toenail
& we'll hang by the Cliffs of Indwell like a red sail

or windmill.
If summer is an image of a string of pearls,
there is singing everywhere.

SONGS

Big fat man skates on thin ice
he cuts a figure eighty-eight
sings, "This is news of Paradise"

I owe my success to the right
bank. & remembering
who didn't sing, sank.

The battleship "Polysemous"
the goodship "Paradise Newes"
the birds, the bees & the frigates

& the lyrics eighty-eight
know what wax works. The
ship of state "Poetics"

like a pulled tooth,
sails up the river, down the
river, twice

It skips, skates, sketches
on the barricades, lyrics
news like lyrics. Newes

# TRANSLATION IS THE SHADOW OF PARADISE

1.
I like your kinky hair. I like the way you talk.
I like the way you walk. I like the way you smell.
I like the whites of your eyes. They're parodies

built in. I like your hotel. Baby, things are going well.
& if I were King of the Jews, I'd call you Sheba.
Lord! I get weak in the knees just thinking of the fire

the real fire of our real lives, my darling girl.
& if the "formula that works" is just another fiction,
I'd settle for dyin' laughin' anywhere with you.

2.

Natural man is a bum, the firemen tell us as they row by
in August, garnering the vote, accolades of water
They row by wearing overcoats & red sails. If Henri
Rousseau had painted a portrait of Fiorello La Guardia
we'd be all set, I feel. Tinhorn funerals, music
like newsreels, wreaths, clocks & badges of flowers, Balinese
& perfectly remembered. & Jimmy Walker tapdancing, the last
Dalmatian puppy, skin coordinate, a string of pearls, lucky

In my state all can have the vote. The express train
to Coney would be a fire engine. Lanterns
would hang on trees, like Aristotle's magic philosophies
hooked to the land, every peasant's Paradise
For, I'm told, the wit of the moon & state hang vice-versa
but Jimmy dances an invention of fireflies, like
so many black & white spots before my eyes
They do deceive me. They stand by the Harbin Inn, rowing

AUG. 4


Alice, Jane & John Adams were sentenced today
in criminal court, on revolutionary steps, the moon's perfect complement

or counterfeit.
The law is august, the months Caesars.
On Foley Square Jesus strings 12 pearls. & cities like Rochester are nemesis.

# FROM THE GREEK ANTHOLOGY

Whose baggage from land to land is despair,
Life's voyagers sail a treacherous sea.
Many founder piteously
With fortune at the helm. We keep
a course this way & that, across the deep,
from here to nowhere. And back again.
Blow foul, blow fair
all come to anchor finally in the tomb.
Passengers, armed, we travel from room to room.

AUG. 20TH

whither England
whither France

stalk of the long-legged fly
Pebbles. Playing fields

# THREE POEMS

## 1. BANNERS

Plagiarism & pornography are twins. Philosophy & philology are cousins.
Signs.
Banners.
Conditions.

## 2. PEBBLES. WAVES

Film unwinds illustrating signs religion static birds space
Wheels turn. At center there's flesh
horseshoe-like

## 3. SYLLABLES

The birds reflect the scene. They are a reflection of the scene.
A drop of water on a bird's wing would reflect the whole world.
Listen.
Like firemen the rhythm section is swinging thru the trees.

# CREDO DICTATED TO A TAPE MACHINE

Aegis of birds.
Entelechy of swans. Black & tan
rhythm section.
        Conic
        scholastics. Periscopes, telescopes &
        phylacteries.
                "White buildings". Swans, I swear.
                Sailors. Infernal
                twin peaks. Canyons. Cities.

## POEM IN THE ROUGH

In the Bronx one still sees Vuillard's streets
& under the El's a path for walking, from dark to light
an elegy of place in & out the contemporary stasis
The bedsheet was folded & put away like a poster

& here in Brooklyn, where the bushes strangle me
for summer's sake, the city, birds, meaning
bats & flowering bees, cantos are born at dawn
Like sheep the flag folds cross-eyed, & whispers, "Church".

CASINOS

The click of castanets, chips, plastic mac & whip girls, who fumbled Versailles
the sound of dice, like rattlesnakes in the desert
& strike against the felt, neither football nor astronauts
Like the thud of certain deaths
Who awakes the stickman, the joys, the rainmaker
when sands and clouds crowd the town
Like soma & fauna & flashes foul—Amen
The flamingo floats in a pool, radio on, a pool
of aquamarine mud ("We only kill each other," Ben Siegel said)
headlights, Massachusetts, roadmaps a pool
In Colorado, one or two weddings, three for journeys
scattered pearls: roadmaps. The strawhatted daughter floats
in the canal connecting isthmus, abyss & architecture—tissue
Another World War. And lucky sons of whisky barons
pure alcohol, pick up chips: chicks placed on windmills (neon skywriting)
Airplanes & machine guns obsolete, the poet's tools:
Tin Pan Alley in the head, the tragicomedy of punctuation, the Great Wall
& mother dead, the face that launched a thousand filmclips—martins—
Old tricks, old tricks: the hat is the triangle in the garden, after all

## ST. MARX IN-THE-BOWERY

it is quite
    immaterial
        what
            consciousness

starts
    to do
        on its own:
            out

        of all such muck
        we get only
                    the
                        one

inference
    that these 3
        moments, the forces
        of production

        the state
                of society
                and conscious-
                    ness

can & must come into
        contradiction
                with
                one another

        because
        the division of
            labor
            implies the possibil-

ity, nay the fact
            that
            intellectual
            & mental

activity—
enjoyment &
        labor, prod-
uction

& consumption—
        devolve on different
        individuals &
        that

        the only possibility
of their not
coming into contradiction
                lies in

        the negation
                in its turn
        of the
        division of labor. It

                is self-
                evident, moreover
                that
                        "specters"

"bonds"
"the higher being"
        "concept"
                "scruple"

are merely the
        idealistic
        spiritual
        expression—

the conception
        of the
        apparently
        isolated individual

      & the image
           of the very
           empirical
    fetters

and limitations
    within which
        the mode
        of the

production of life
        & the form of
        intercourse cou-
    pled with it, move

CRYSTAL CLOWN 1776–1777

Be awake mornings. See the light spread across the lawn. There's a strange lady in my front yard
(snow) as the sky refuses to be any color, today A girl's naked in the shower, saying
"I like this boat-ride I'm being taken for, although "I'm keeping my boxes dry!" A naked artist
It never leaves the shore, this boat. Its fires burn Smoking. Bad teeth. Wooden planks:
Furniture. Sky Like a pair of lovely legs. It's a garage that grew up one minute ago
I stopped thought: 12 years of cops Sometimes I can't talk, my mouth too full of words, but In
my life. & Alice is putting her panties on I have hands & other parts, to talk lots! Light
the fire Takes off a flowery dress for London's purple one Babble to you. I dream a green undersea
Man Out of the blue, a host of words, floating Has been assigned to me, to keep me v.i.p., To
smirk March: awaiting rescue: smoke, or don't At me when I'm being foolish. A not unpleasant dream
Strapped: deprived. Shoot yourself: stay alive. My secret doors open as the mail arrives. Fresh
air & you can't handle yourself, love, feeling Pours in, around, before they close again
The winds are rushing No inclination toward that solitude. Take it easy, & as it comes. Coffee
Up off of the ocean, up Little Plains Road. Catch the Wind Suss. Feel. Whine. Shut up. Exercise
In my head, a quiet song. And, "Everything belongs to me Turn. Turn around. Turn. Kill dog
Because I am poor." Waiting in sexy silence, someone Today woke up bright & early, no mail, life
Now a tiny fire flares out front the fireplace. Chesterfield Is Horrible, & I am stupid, & I think
Nothing . . . King lights up! Wood is crackling inside "Have faith, old brother. You are a myth
in my heart Elephants' rush & roar. Refrigerator's gentle drone. Sounds in dreams In bed You are
all there is inside my head. We are both alive. Imagined footsteps moving toward my door, & India

THUMBS (The White Jew)

"Orangutans are skeptical of changes/In their cages"
Hemingway sat in a barn & wrote, composing
fear, World War 2, the whiskey bottle; the blast, the blast
that shook the scenery, & typewriter, too. He gave the prize
to Pound, & left town; Havana. He wasn't a Jew
& lost—this is apocryphal—
when he thumb-wrestled T.C. Jones, or was it Oppenheimer, or Oppen
who also ran. You see, the prize was Marlene D., Norman's friend—
Indeed; a man must love, & blow his brains out
& Ford Madox Ford will survive *A Moveable Feast*
that cross between a tophat & sonnet, wherein, white as money
the belly of the whale is Turgenev's *Bezhin Meadow*
The lights went out, know ye by these here presentiments
& Huck Finn & *A Sportsman's Notebook* were 2 works he loved

# A TEXT FOR A FOUND PHOTOGRAPH

I lift satin or velvet/feeling you unable to touch me/my come on yr tits
Or denim under it is/I think of the times/tug at the hair of
always your pubic/that you did/feeling yr snatch feel/thatch

Of hair and/you pull from my touch/yr lips on/The lips are wet
i think of the times you suck my cock/I think of the times/body, my legs &
your ass and cunt are/that you didn't/i think my cock/feel my cock

Of the times i covered/stuffed with vibrators/push inside you/feel
your hands and feet/you with both myself and/You rise to that
outstretched, your/my come, and I think/touching, feel you make

Eyes are closed, your/now That you did not like/me rise to your
breasts have ropes/it, but I did not know/touching, find Ourselves
tying life & death/Across them

You shudder/that them/i thought/as you come/It was a gift
only yr due/The dark night in/which is flesh & which is fantasy
and ecstasy & fear/Which is the other self/Changes in me/or in my Love

toe, with a touch, Of us heat & heart/i do not know why I knot
The blame/the house, the lust
touches meet again/When once you pulled me To you/eyes, sweat/Overhead & rent

## ANECDOTE

In the paradise they played in they lit three on a match
contradanced non-musical chairs in their bird-of-feather paradise
Now, no device of their own contrition can welcome or harbor
lo! their vessel upon the waters. She betrayed her husband
he his friend a season's evening when, light upon light
a switch was pulled, & the Christmas-tree city, lot-cast
charred, burned, lit up along its strewn black ways, districts
a harlot-swine's string of pearls. The day's retreat, "All's
deprived or stolen," sounded hollow, unechoed in the street
No joy was wed to mystery. A silt-like rain began. Wet, unwashed, &
lacking fare, they stand, stay in the gardened, rain-soaked air
wishing there still might come a dove, wish for it as they never
wished for love, cess, peace, the green leaf of their survival
something to repair. Blurred neon trinities & bowlers inform the
Air. They stand, it seems, for seven nights. From New Mexico
I hear there's only pastel Spring, & things must grow tough
to grow green. He's neither grey nor green, still plays the leaping

.    .    .    .    .    .    .    .    .

.    .    .    .    .    .    .    .    .

On highways to the Temporary. Or, fragment, say can't you see?

## JANUARY SONG

The rain comes down
Umbrellas go up
The rain goes
*Pup! pup! pup!*

I'll weep, I'll weep
& when I've wept I'll weep.
Tears are  tears.
I'll weep typewriters.

Don't weep, sweep.
Phones, too, are mirrors.
The moon is bloody.
Don't weep, sweep.

Sleep.  Twin signets—alba
& vespers—are twilight's coin.
The double-axe spins
last year & this.  Sleep.

ELUARD'S

Every medal is false; diamonds, too
Weapons of slumber are hallowed in the night
Picasso was here, cheerily dressed
Under the bursting sky the earth is invisible

The face of the heart loses color
The sun seeks us, snowblind
We gave the horizon our wings'
Archaic stage; & our gaze dissipates error

# AN ALBUM OF WORDS FOR S.

Sarong, the labyrinth, the needle's I, blue newsreels
Place de la Place, amerika, penguins, lobsters
camels, elephants, the Works, the Werkes
The States, Gunther Din, *Dombey & Son*
calypsos, Saxophones, labyrinths, lobotomies
cures, Spas, classifieds, Information, tourism, The End
beginning with a line by Pirandello: curses
Shirts, lemons, sestinas,  seashells, marguerites
pacifics, price tags, rumors, dust, Gold
mohammedan Bo Peeps, birthdays, alphabets, washing
Machines, cities, Arks, arc, oceans, lemons, literature
revolution, Alps, Pyrenees, piranas, pianos
past, future & Perfect, liberation, the Paris Commune
the Pope, pop, Pope, amen, the Paris Commune, lemons, metros
Dictionaries, dichotomies, diagram, dogs, Chinese
sampans, Dixie, doxies, dachshunds, *daseins*, Ampersands, scampi
duets, Dues, cats, Eats, Fidelio, der Rosenkavalier, pop, pop, pop
Demerest, dublin, Dorchester, diagram, diaphragm, dust, Duse
pelicans, puffins, parliaments, preterites, Poughkeepsie
peking, Palm Beach, Pennsylvania, colorado, Alaska
Altona; circumstance, circumcised, circumcised, Bakunin, dust
anarchist, Phi Beta Kappa, diametric, Pola, pinkerton, past
proletarian, prostitutes, pimps, ping-pong, Poe
the Great Wall, boulder, St. George, anachronism, rhythm, etc. Days

## NOVEL

Now a transvestite revue
now an orgy
now a nightmare
now a painting of parrot-like brilliance
now a voodoo ceremony
now a medical operation
now a subway trip
now an excursion with a motorcycle gang
now a sequence of homosexual lyrics
now rude
now superb
now punning & playful
now a satire on jet-age mysticism
now an orgy
now a blank page
now a nightmare
now an evocation of Oriental wonders

now a cobra
now a pup
now a tundra
now a totem

## PUSHKIN'S LYRIC

I've survived aspiration
      fancy disdain
Hollowheartedness
        & suffering remain

. . . Fate crowned me
with bay leaves
      I want to die
Mostly, I'm lonely)

      In the beginning
struck by the cold
        All seasons are Winter
        leaf-naked, etc.

## THE SEAFARER (Anglo-Saxon)

For pastime the gannet's cry served me, & the kittiwake's chatter,
The roar of the sea, ice-cold waves, & the song of the swans.
For laughter of men, for mead-drink, the call of the sea-mews.
Hail flew in showers around me, & I heard what I could
In wretchedness, robbed of my kinsmen, with icicles hung.
On the ice-cold sea I passed the winter in exile;
And hunger within me, sea-wearied, made havoc of courage.
This he, whose lot chances happily on land, doesn't know.
Yet hotly were wailing the querulous sighs round my heart, tho
My feet were imprisoned in frost, & fettered with ice-chains.
At the prow of my craft as it tossed under the cliffs,
Benumbed by the cold, oft the comfortless nightwatch held me.

# AUTUMN TRANSLATION FROM THE JAPANESE

Rain beats on rain

—

Birds cry, mountain
        silences deepen
                Wind subsiding

                The flowers still fall

The long night:
        The sound of water
                Says what I think

On a withered branch
        A crow, perched
                In the autumn evening

The stars on the pond
        A winter shower
        Again ruffles the water

A trout leaps, solo—
        Clouds are moving
                In the bed of the stream

The skylark:
        Its voice alone
        leaves nothing behind

What is being shouted
        In the dense mist
                between the hills?

The sea darkens
        The voices of the white ducks
                Are faintly white

The stream hides itself
        In the grasses
                Of departing autumn

Rain beats on rain
        Falling leaves
                Lie on one another

The thief ate a peach—
        left the moon at the window
                Rain writes the poem

The falling leaf
                returning to the branch
                Was a butterfly

# OUR TRIP TO INDIA

about diagonals, diagonal angles, diagonal glances
about eyes that never meet
about three-quarter spaces
about the sound of closing doors
about footsteps

about the sound of water
about the sound of glass
about glances
about death in our midst

about light falling on faces
about light in the dark, falling on faces
about blood on the forehead
about a white crepe blouse, unheard records

about blue
about flowers picked & not taken home with you
about cars, roaring animals, roaring motorcycles
about green
about hands

about pride
about bourgeois pride, about jealousy
about stopped light
about brown & yellow
about yellow

about indirect glances
about doors opening & closing
about looking in & not seeing in
about hope, about a window
about a red car seat, a red window

about a green bed & green curtains
about standing behind a door
about a smile
about eyes
about metal

about sleep
about two diagonals

& a poem is a paragraph
& painted Venus because she didn't exist
& spatialized Aristotle's "plot"
& threw his pocket watch across the Hoboken River
& chopped down Chekhov's *The Cherry Orchard*
& launched a thousand film clips
& rose against the wind, like fish falling
& now my wits & ribs sing, not my bones

& all the guys who never made it
& all the guys who made it
& all the women who waited
& those dead in the wars
& those murdered in their poverty
& all the new nations, successful tribes
& all the Mohammedans & their dreams of glory

& the radical journalists who fed me news
& now my wits & ribs sing, not my bones
& the scribes, utopians & passionate conservatives
& the revolutionary anarchists, black or apostolic
& Frankie Frisch, & Franklin P. Adams
& Lao-Tze, Marc Schleifer & Malcolm X, especially
May they breathe eternity, & roar like me
a three-dimensional body

Hear my song

## RETRIEVAL

the girl, the garden, the image, 2 dogs, off the log
Brooklyn tits are myths, "heavily-weighted" titles
A Rip Van Winkle by Dumas awakes in the Smolny Institute
The Chinese's dream, & the butterfly's dream—
both are clapping. Blackest day. An afternoon
with Breton & Tzara near the Eiffel Tower. A carriage
passes: Lenin, Lautrec & Bolshoi ballerinas
waving flags are within, a chanteuse's chessgame
in progress. A shot rings out, wounds the scribe
previously a painter. At the tableau's center: a unicorn
limousine. Proust unwinds like a resurrected mummy
A corkscrew pops, & agencies are born, blue siphons
blondes, & Americans. The day after the revolution, '89
IBM's doors open the other way. Godard prays: Colette
is his nightmare, as if Ben Franklin were alive, as if
he were the folk bard of the Nile-Congo divide! Prod-
Producers smoke cigars, even as poets do. They are called
Apollinaires. Her turnover in men & jewelry was great
her hips were huge, like motion pix, the biological actress
& mistress of an age. My scenarios are not flocks, my
cameras are not high-heeled mirrors. Three forces
brothers & sisters, unwind in slow motion—because
it is there, & because a cut is a dissolve—like Alps
or Pyrenees, & the whole boatload of atmospheric pudding
& the question was asked, "Who killed the slow mambo?"
& "Where is Dave Antin now?" Beauty! Old Pastoral!
Mona, moustachio'd, walks on stiletto heels. On the
Metro, the pond, the mall, the playing fields of baseball
I carry the work upstairs. They dance the famous hornpipe
in moonlight. In January my daddy threw water at me
Piano keys are murder mysteries. I'm going to Alabama
with a bandaid on my knee. & Kansas City, & Kansas City

POET AND FILMMAKER FRANK KUENSTLER was born in Havana in 1928, lived in New York City, died there in 1996. He was the author of *Lens* (1964), *Selected Poems* (1964), *Paradise News* (1966), *Fugitives. Rounds* (1966), *13½ Poems* (1984), *Continued* (1987), *Miscellany* (1987), *In Which* (1994), and *The Seafarer, B.Q.E., and Other Poems* (1996). His work appeared in *The Nation*, *The Village Voice*, and *Film Culture*, in many little magazines, and in the anthologies *Mixed Voices* and *America: A Prophecy*. His poems were translated into Russian and Italian. His films include *Color Idioms* and the august *El Atlantis*. He taught at the School of Visual Arts, edited *Bread&* and *Airplane*, and was one of the animating spirits of The Eventorium, an arts collective on Manhattan's upper west side.